Dancing with GOD

Through the Evening of Life

Reflections From a Dying Man

by Mary Anne McCrickard Benas

St. Pius X Church
P.O. Box 310
209 S. Williams
Moberly, MO 65270

Unless otherwise noted all Scripture quotations are from the New American Bible, Copyright 1970 by the Confraternity of Christian Doctrine, Washington, D.C. 20017. Used with permission.

ISBN # 0-9648448-2-6
Library of Congress Catalog Card Number # 96-072240

Copyright© 1998 MaryAnne McCrickland Benas

All rights reserved.
No part of this book may be used or reproduced in any manner whatsoever without written permission.

Manufactured in the United States of America

CMJ Marian Publishers
P.O. Box 661, Oak Lawn, Illinois 60454
www.cmjbooks.com

Dedication

To my elderly friend, John, who truly dances with God through all the seasons of life and teaches us how to embrace the twilight years.

Table of Contents

Acknowledgments ix

Dancing with God xi

Foreword xiii

Introduction xvii

"I'm Dying — You Know!" 1

God is Our Playmate 4

Prayers of A Soul 7

Thank You, God 9

The Joy of Giving and Receiving 11

Waiting with Hope 13

The Lord's Servant 17

Laughter — The Best Medicine 19

Riches in Heaven 21

v

God Loves A Humble Heart 22

85 Years Young 24

The Secret to Success 26

"Everything I Have Is Yours!" 28

To Rest in God 30

My Crucifix 33

Why Does Our Time Together Have To Be So Short? .. 35

God As Trickster 37

Dancing In Our Hearts 40

Live Out the Dream 41

Just A Big Kid 43

A Weed is the Best 45

In the Very Heart of God 46

I Will Always Be With You 48

Showers of Love 50

The Tenderness of God 51

May I Say a Few Words, God?........................53

"Be Near Me"..................................55

The Gathering..................................56

The Path to God................................60

The Power of Prayer............................62

God of Celebrations............................67

I Will See You — Soon!.........................69

Dad's In Heaven................................71

The Spirit Continues to Dance..................73

Join in the Dance of Compassion................76

The Ageless Dance of Love......................78

Epilogue – What Can A Dying Person Give?.......80

Grand Finale – The Eternal Shuffle.............82

Notes..84

Acknowledgments

Let us rejoice in Our Creator's delightful sense of humor and how God is forever revealing Himself in the most surprising and unexpected ways. God's Spirit of Love and Laughter often leads us in new directions that are not our own choosing. For example, as my husband and I dreamt of a family, I needed to leave my teaching job to pursue extensive doctoring at a fertility center. As my heart longed for a child and my whole being waited to conceive and give birth, I met an 85 year old man through the hospice program whose heart longed to see the face of God, whose whole being was waiting to die. It was then that I discovered that birthing and dying are really very similar. I was feeling very sad – very dead on the inside, but my friend's spirit was very joyful. Meeting John was a life-giving and empowering experience. It is with a spirit of gratitude and thankfulness that this book was written. In the sharing of this story with others, my tears have been turned into laughter and my sorrow has become a joyful dance. Truly, when our hearts are filled with gratitude, we see God everywhere.

In the midst of his old age and illness, John prayed to the Blessed Virgin, Mother of God, that she would send someone to comfort him while he was dying. All the chaplains, doctors, nurses, nurse's aides, and caregivers were the answer to that prayer. All those involved in the hospice program are, indeed, a sign of God's presence.

ACKNOWLEDGEMENTS

<u>Therefore, all proceeds from the sale of this book, that would normally go to the author, will go to hospice or other organizations that service the elderly and the dying.</u> Concerning the nurse who helped care for him, John said: "**When we get together, we laugh like a couple of 14-year olds.**" To me, John said: "**God brought us together. Jesus is loving us; Jesus is smiling and laughing.**"

Let us acknowledge the constant devotion of all family members and friends who help a loved one approach death with dignity and self-respect. With regard to his relatives, John said: "**My family is so good to me and I love them all.**"

A loving thanks to my husband, John Benas, who believed in my dream. Through his deep faith, patience, positive energy and wonderful computer skills, this book became a reality. It is only due to my husband's love and understanding that I had the opportunity and the time to write the following pages.

A special thanks to my parents, Art and Helen McCrickard, who planted the seeds of faith within me, and to God who helped them to grow.

The encouragement and support of friends who proofread the book and offered many helpful suggestions is greatly appreciated. These included Gail and Owen Hilding, Jeanne Jerousek, Diane Massura, Cathy and Tim Meaney, Jane Rowley and Deedee Van Dyke.

Dancing with God

Oh, to dance with God the Beloved of our soul,
To flow with the changing seasons and be made whole.

To move with the rhythm of birth, death and rebirth,
In the midst of merrymaking and playful mirth.

To soar through the evening of life when day is done,
Frolicking with Our Heart's Delight in new found fun.

With high spirits and joy let's kick up our heels,
Amid wondrous music and candlelight meals.

To laugh in wild abandon with lively cheers,
To tap dance and leap through shadows of needless fears.

In our innermost being, the Great Dance vibrates.
Activating new visions, the soul celebrates.

Put on our dancing shoes; untangle guilt and pain,
With a tip of the hat and a twirl of the cane.

Let's lovingly waltz right into God's warm embrace,
Dancing in the very heart of God with truest grace.

Mary Anne McCrickard Benas

Foreword

Where are we in the dance of life? Are we stumbling, falling, following, leading, gliding or soaring? Is the dance a slow steady trot or a fast-paced jig? Do we tap dance around our problems, or can we waltz right through our pain? Are we flowing in harmony, moving to the tune of God's plan by uniting our lives with the celebration?

During mass, a three year old child turned to his mother, raised his arms and said: "I want to go up. I want to see Jesus. I want to see Jesus close up." His mother smiled, bent down, lovingly lifted her son and held him in her arms. With eyes of wonder, the child gazed at the cross, the altar and the Eucharist. He looked into the eyes of the priest, the congregation and listened intently to the Word, the music — seeing Christ everywhere.

In the celebration of all that life is, can we bring our gifts, joys, sorrows, fears, hopes and dreams to God? Can we "see Jesus close up" in the day to day events of life? This book proclaims an incredible faith journey which reveals that even in the midst of death — even at this stage of life, we can still reach out and touch one another. John's story of God will give us a vivid glimpse of death filled with such hope and promise, that we will feel as if we already have one foot in heaven. This book is a collection of daily reflections and meditations to help our lives become a living prayer.

John would pray and talk to God in such a genuine and heartwarming way. One day John prayed: **"Dear**

God, I will not be on earth much longer. Come to my home and bring your friends. We have plenty of food. You can help yourself to some coffee. Dear God, I am asking you and your friends to come to my home so that I can begin to feel at home with you, and then one day I will be ready to go to your home. I hear you have a wonderful meal prepared, a true feast waiting for me. Forgive me, God, but I am feeling a bit afraid to come to you. God, please give me the grace I need so that I can come to you." Can we also embrace the Spirit and join in the ageless dance of love?

Only the Spirit understands how one person's life impacts another. One afternoon, an eight year old boy named Charlie joyfully announces: "Mom, we're having a fund raiser at school. I'm supposed to get magazine subscriptions." His Mom thinks: "Oh no, another fund raiser." Seeing the sparkle in her son's eyes, feeling his excitement, she intuitively senses that this is a teachable moment, for there is a level of readiness. His Mom explains: "Charlie, I'm reading a book about a man named John. He was very old, and sick and was dying. He was an extremely successful business man. One story is called, 'The Secret to Success.' Would you like to learn his secret?" Charlie eagerly nods his head, sits down to listen and seems to be absorbing the story like a sponge.

John's words ring true: **"Here's the secret to a successful business. Every night I would get down on my knees and pray: 'Lord, I don't have the answer to this problem; but you have all the answers. Please help me! Give me a sign! Tell me what you want me to do!'"** After hearing the story Charlie exclaims, "Wow!" He promptly kneels, bows his head, folds his hands and prays silently to God. When he is finished, his Mom explains: "That's right, Charlie. Praying is the faith part. Now, you need to do the work part." She proceeds to explain that a friend of the family who is a doctor has many magazines in his office. They discuss other friends and relatives who might be interested. It would have been so easy for her to simply make the contacts, but she encourages her son to make the calls. Charlie plans what he will say, musters up his courage, then picks up the phone ready to tackle the "work part."

With forty six magazine subscriptions, Charlie is the winner! He shares the good news with his Mom: "Everyone applauded me! I'm going to get a limo ride with the principal to a restaurant. We're going to have lunch together. Everyone wanted to know my secret. I didn't tell them, because then they would win, too!" His Mom laughs and says: "Charlie, you have to share the secret." For as John said: **"Now I would like to pass my business on to you! Just remember, as long as you are into the power and glory of God, you are in the right business."**

The words of an eighty five year old man are deeply influencing an eight year old child. Perhaps, this book reveals the true secret to happiness. For as John said: **"Making contact with God, making contact with people – that is what life is all about. That is what I try to do!"** May the same Spirit of God dance in our souls, so we too can sparkle with heartfelt love.

Introduction

A PRIEST ONCE SHARED A STORY: "Ann used to be the belle of the party, the star dancer. When she danced, the crowd parted like the Red Sea and stood back and watched with awe. The crowd would clap, cheer and whistle as she danced. Men would fight over her, and cut in on each other. When she danced, she was vivacious, dazzling and stunning with her sparkling, radiant eyes.

"Now Ann's hair is gray; her face is wrinkled with age. Her arms and hands that once looked so graceful as she twirled and spun around are crippled due to arthritis. Her legs are like tree trunks, for she can hardly move.

"All of Ann's dancing partners are dead; she has outlived her husband, family and friends. She is all alone; at times she even feels as if God has abandoned her. Ann's eyes that once sparkled and radiated with joy and laughter are now dull and lifeless. She stares at the four walls, talks to the TV set and waits to die."*

So many stories left untold. So many tears that never dried. I often wondered: how can such despair be turned into hope? How can such loneliness be turned into love? How can such tears be turned into laughter?

Then I met a man whose story of God revealed an alternative to despair. My friend John, who was in his eighties and had cancer, was approaching death as if it were a work of art. Yes, he felt the pain, wrestled with the struggle, experienced the loneliness, and groped in dark-

---

* **Used with permission.**

ness with the emptiness; truly, my friend encountered his own agony in the garden. Yet, even in the midst of great suffering, he was very aware of God's presence. Due to his tremendous faith, he died just as he had lived — loving, laughing, praising the Lord and celebrating life — but first he confronted his own brokenness.

John's most frequent words as he was dying were: **"I don't know what to do. No one knows what to do. You would think someone would know, but no one knows what to do."** When John came to the end of his strength, when he cried out in pain and was brought to his knees, when he felt completely helpless and powerless — perhaps such a time provided the space and room for the Spirit of God to dance. Every person who is physically dying, each individual who is grieving over the death of a loved one, everyone who is dying to an old way of existing so new life can emerge, has possibly had a similar experience. The purpose of this book is to reach out to all those who are wrestling with the painful reality of death. It is my hope that John's story of God will help each of us discover and become more aware of our own stories of God. Perhaps we can all find comfort in St. Paul's words:

> *"I willingly boast of my weaknesses instead,*
> *that the power of Christ may rest upon me....*
> *when I am powerless, it is then that I am strong"*
> *(2 Corinthians 12:9-10).*

In the midst of feeling powerless, how can a person approach death as if it were a work of art? John's secret is revealed in this Scripture passage:

*"Hoping for what we cannot see
means awaiting it with patient endurance.
The Spirit too helps us in our weakness,
for we do not know how to pray as we ought;
but the Spirit himself makes intercession for us
with groanings that cannot be expressed in
speech"* (Romans 8:25-26).

John's prayer was: **"Dear God, I don't know how to pray as I should. Let me be quiet and still, so that you can pray through me."** John truly knew how to rest in God, so he was touching Spirit all the time.

It was, indeed, the Spirit of God that brought John and me together. As a 37-year old volunteer chaplain in the hospice program, I visited John, an 85-year old man, for a period of five months before he died. I found his words so inspiring and extraordinary that I began journaling each visit as a keepsake for myself. When I realized that John was not able to remember his own wonderful words from day to day due to the cancer and medication, I began to give him copies of the prayers and thoughts he had shared with me. John seemed to enjoy reading his words, laughing at his own wit and marveling at his own wisdom. On a retreat and during Communion services, I often shared some of John's insights with others and discovered that his story was touching people very deeply. I remember when John greeted me one morning with: **"What did you find out about our book — the book we are writing?"** It seemed that those words were meant to be turned into a reality.

This book is a collection of sayings and thoughts of

a dying man with a rich spiritual perspective. In order to distinguish between John's words and my own thoughts and feelings when I was with him, all of **<u>John's actual words are in bold print</u>** while everything else is added by me, the chaplain, for further reflection. John's words are simple, pure and earthy yet deeply profound. Truly, it is in the ordinary and the concrete that we encounter the sacred; and there is nothing more concrete than hospital beds, cans of Ensure, bed pans and enemas.

Some of the essays contain a dialogue between God and a soul. It seemed that the best way to portray the struggle, irony and paradox was to have John and God wrestling, laughing and crying out together. By confronting the pain, our sorrow can become a dance. Referring to his own old age, illness and approaching death, John once said: **"Oh, everything is such a muddle; still, God is here, somewhere."** The light of God is indeed greater than the darkness of our human experience. That is why we need to dance with Our Maker at all times, but especially in the evening of life.

The dance of life can be fast, slow, wild, or peaceful. At times we stumble, fall and miss the beat; but God, Our Dancing Partner, is forever hugging, leading, guiding and even carrying us. John loved to dance, and may the music of his soul help us discover and become more aware of the same Life-giving Spirit that promenades right through our human frailty in true glory. I pray that the tenderness of God will dance inside each of us as we read John's words, so we too can freely move with the seasons of our lives and embrace the cycles of birthing, dying and rebirthing that we experience. Then one day, we will also be able to leap into the twilight years of life — filled with hope and promise.

Let us celebrate all the changing rhythms of life. A man who had been friends with John for over fifty years said to me: "You've only known John when he was sick, but I knew him in his prime. He was amazing. Why, you never even saw him dance!" Yet, when John was sick, he was at his spiritual prime and was dancing with God with renewed life and vitality. Can we begin to discover that we do, indeed, experience the divine even in the midst of pain and sadness? Can we respond to the inner call of Our Eternal God who gently nudges us in the midst of all the ups and downs of life, and lovingly asks: "May I have this dance?" As Scripture says:

> *"You have changed my sadness into a joyful dance;*
> *you have taken away my sorrow*
> *and surrounded me with joy.*
> *So I will not be silent;*
> *I will sing praise to you.*
> *LORD, you are my God;*
> *I will give you thanks forever" (Psalm 30:11-12).*[1]

If we can all sing this song of praise, then we will be able to plunge into the wonder, beauty and mystery of it all in true humility.

Ultimately, there are no words, techniques or procedures that can adequately prepare us for the letting go that is a part of dying. Age, medical advice and even life experience do not equip us for that total trust and complete surrender that is so necessary at the moment of death. Any endeavors we have achieved or accomplished in life seem very small in comparison to the power and glory of God. Perhaps all we can do is place our life humbly in God's hands. To Our All-powerful, Awesome God, John often prayed: **"I'm just a stupid human. God, I'm afraid to come to you — <u>you're God</u>. Please give me the grace I need so that I can come to you."**

How can we let go of such human fears and open our hearts to God's grace? Once a 4 year old child parted with her bunny rabbit in the hopes of giving grandma some comfort before her surgery the next morning. On another occasion, a woman while giving birth asked her husband to hold up a picture of their two year old son to remind her "what it's all about." Then, there was an elderly woman who started making toy dolls for newborn babies as she was dying of cancer. An old, torn up bunny rabbit, a photograph, even a toy doll can become almost sacred when they are given in a great outpouring of love. Can we allow this Spirit of Love which sparkles even in the darkest hours to transform our fears into faith? Could it be that it takes death to teach us about life?

"I'm Dying — You Know!"

"I'M 85 YEARS OLD; so if I'm forgetful, you'll have to be patient! I'm still young enough to admire an attractive woman. I see beauty in everything and everyone.

"I'm dying — you know!

"When I was a child, a priest said, 'John, you would make a wonderful priest. Are you interested? Would you like to be a priest?' I replied, 'Sure, okay!' I joined the seminary only to discover that it wasn't for me; however, my faith was always an important and vital part of my life.

"I'm dying — you know!

"I married and was involved with my family, my work, our parish and community. I was president of this committee and that committee. Now I'm slowing down; I'm old, sick and tired.

"I'm dying — you know!

"I traveled around the world with my wife. Now, I'm coming to the end of my journey.

"I'm dying — you know!

"My wife died a year ago, last May first. I cared for her when she was sick and dying.

"I'm dying — you know!

"This young man who lives with me and helps care for me is a good person. My daughter hired him. Even though this man is always with me, I still feel so alone.

I wish my wife was sleeping beside me and at home with me.

"I'm dying — you know!

"The other night at the party, I danced with a sparkle in my eyes and a cane in my hands, for I felt fully alive.

"I'm dying — you know!

"Once a week a high school student visits me and we play checkers. I try to help him prepare for his future and guide him in choosing a career that's right for his strengths and talents.

"I'm dying — you know!

"Did we laugh together? Did I bring a smile to your face? When will I see you again? Thursday? Oh, I'll try to stay alive until then, so I can see you again.

"I'm dying — you know!"

As we reflect on our lives, can we let the words **"I'm dying — you know"** echo inside of us, and become more aware of our own feelings towards death? Can we discover how our stories of God commingle with the Great Story of Christ's Resurrection? Can the joyful, sorrowful and glorious mysteries of our lives become one with the joyful, sorrowful and glorious mysteries of Jesus' life? Can we begin to realize that we all experience the cycles of death and resurrection, not only at the end of our physical life, but each and every day? We each need to:

"Die to I – so there can be we.

Die to 'give me' – so we can have.

Die to our fears – so we can love.

Die to self-centeredness – so we can build community.

Perhaps we die a bit each day in order to truly live."[2]

When at last we return home to the tender and loving embrace of Our Creator, He will say: "You are my delight! You have deeply shared the gift of your life with others. Look at how you can love and laugh. Thanks for a job well done, my good and faithful servant!"

God Is Our Playmate

GOD HAS FUN simply being with each of us, and even plays with humanity as scripture reveals:

> "I (Spirit of Wisdom) was his (God's) delight day by day,
> playing before him all the while,
> playing on the surface of his earth;
> and I found delight in the children of men"
> (Proverbs 8:30-31).

As Co-creator, the Spirit danced side by side with Yahweh — giving birth to the earth, the world, the cosmos. The Playful Spirit danced with vibrance, exuberance, spontaneity and imagination — generating new life and energy.

Down through the ages, the image of God as Playmate has frequently been used. Mechtild of Magdeburg, a mystic in the thirteenth century, had a vision of God in which Our Creator said to her: "I, God, am your playmate! I will lead the child in you in wonderful ways for I have chosen you"[3] to join the dance. We are filled with so many fears and worries, that we are unable to hear the music. We get tangled up in so much guilt and pain, that we miss the dance.

Let us continually dance and play with God, Our Heart's Delight, but especially during the darkness of the twilight years — for all of life is a playground. Can we approach even death skipping with God, with spirits soaring, leaping and frolicking? God, Our Playmate, joyfully shouts to each of us:

> "I will restore you, and you shall be rebuilt...
> Carrying your festive tambourines,
> you shall go forth dancing with the merrymakers"
> (Jeremiah 31:4).

Can we let the inner child come out and play and be genuine, honest and real, putting on no pretenses? Can we put our thumb on our nose and wiggle our fingers at authority, because we have discovered our own inner authority which is rooted in God? Can we leapfrog over problems and difficulties one at a time? On the monkey bars of life, can we trust the rhythm and jump from one hand to the other, swinging right through our fears and worries with a carefree spirit? Let us celebrate the game of Hide and Seek and how God reveals Himself when we least expect it. God is always seeking us out and knocking on our hearts. He will find us no matter where we hide, for God loves the game of Hide and Seek! Can we laugh at ourselves, not take ourselves so seriously and jokingly say: **"My mind, my mind, where art thou?"**

Surely there have been moments when we each knew how to play and dance with God from the darkness of human suffering to the light of grace. Our God says: "My child, when you are ready, come home to me; then you will dance and dance and never grow tired. The surprise ending of death is that there is no end, only a beginning – the resurrection of the soul. I promise you an <u>ever-</u>

laughing life, I mean _everlasting life_. Oh, my mind, my mind, where art thou?"

Prayers of A Soul

(This essay was written in response to some of the questions with which John was struggling, in hope of giving him some comfort. The dialogue between God and a Soul is meant to portray the turmoil, irony and paradox of it all.)

VOICE OF A SOUL:
"MY LIFE USED TO be rich with meaning, for I was involved with my wife, children, career, Church and community. I was president of this committee and that committee. Now I'm weak, I'm tired and I can't move much. I'm the most confused man in the world; it's hard to have fun with people when I can't remember things. I'm dying, you know; so I say to God: 'What meaning does my life have now?'"

VOICE OF GOD:
"I see the overall picture, so don't worry about the details. Just trust the process, as my love unfolds with all the beauty of a rose."

VOICE OF A SOUL:
"At times, I'm in such pain. Why does dying have to hurt so?"

VOICE OF GOD:
"Suffering is a lot like garbage. At first it is disgusting

and repulsive in every way; but it makes great fertilizer, and really helps things to grow."[4]

VOICE OF A SOUL:
"I feel so useless, so powerless! I've lived too long!"

VOICE OF GOD:
"Now is the time to tap into the <u>Power of God</u> to be <u>empowered,</u> so you can truly live."

VOICE OF A SOUL:
"When my wife died, I was so lonely; there was such a void, an emptiness. Now, I'm dying. I prayed to the Blessed Virgin, Mother of God, that she would send someone to comfort me while I'm dying. I prayed for a hand to hold, someone to listen to all my stories. Oh, isn't it time for a hug? Oh, this is wonderful!"

VOICE OF GOD:
"My Precious One, soon your heart will sing anew and your spirit will truly soar, for the dance goes on and never, ever dies. I, the Lord of the Dance, will teach you some new moves that will knock your socks off. Just remember that some days are baby-step days, until at long last you join the Great Dance."

Thank You, God

LET OUR WHOLE BEING REJOICE in Our Gracious God.

*"Take delight in the LORD,
and he will grant you your heart's requests"
(Psalm 37:4).*

With heartfelt joy, John prayed: **"Thank you, God, for giving us the gift of life; but we don't always know what to do with our life. You have to tell us what you want us to do, and we have to listen.**

"Thank you, God, for giving us our bodies; but we also need your grace, so we know how to use our bodies. We know that we are to serve others, help someone who is sick, and reach out to someone in need; but we also need to have fun. We turn to you, Lord, because you are the origin of fun. Everything comes from you; so surely, fun must come from you.

"Thank you for my son. As a child he would say: 'I don't want to do this! I don't want to do that!' I prayed to you: 'Lord, what am I going to do with this kid!' I did what you told me to do; I tried to accept him. Now I'm old, sick and dying; but my son accepts me. He is always here and he is fun to have around. Lord, you worked it out so beautifully, so wonderfully.

"We all hope to see you someday. Whether it is short or long before we see you, only you know. I hope

I'm not boring you, but let me say it again: thank you, God, for life. I pray that the last words on my lips as I die will be: 'Thank you, God, for the gift of life.'"

Can we all meet Our Creator with a grateful, trusting heart? As Our Maker's plan begins to unfold in our lives, Our Ever-present God promises:

> *"I know well the plans I have in mind for you...*
> *plans to give you a future full of hope.*
> *When you call me,*
> *when you go to pray to me,*
> *I will listen to you.*
> *When you look for me,*
> *you will find me.*
> *Yes, when you seek me with all your heart,*
> *you will find me with you"* (Jeremiah 29:11-14).

Let us give thanks to Our Generous God who fills our void with simple, loving moments and constantly provides us with the gifts we need.

The Joy of Giving and Receiving

ONE MORNING, John had his glasses on and pointed to the tip of my nose and asked, "What's that?" I laughed and replied: "It's a freckle. A friend of mine jokingly says that every freckle means I was kissed by an angel. I guess that was a great big kiss." John roared with laughter and said: **"We should peel it off, hang it up on the wall and award it World's Biggest Freckle."**

Still laughing, John asked: **"What does your heart desire? What can I do for you?"** I replied: "Well, my husband and I long to have a family. You can pray for us, John."

He tenderly and lovingly cradled my left hand between his two hands while raising it to heaven and prayed life-giving words: **"Dear God, she has brought such comfort and peace to me in my last days. Now I want to help her. My prayer, my hope, my wish is that she can have a family. Lord, you are the source of all help; so we turn to you. You have to help her so she can have a child. We know you have everything up there; surely you must have a child you could send down here to us. A child just the way you want him or her to be."** John winked at me, patted my hand and said: **"Consider it done. You've got it. It's all arranged."** We've asked; now we need to wait and receive. John began to sing to the child of my dreams; then he said: **"You can join in the song!"**

Oh, how wondrous to die loving, laughing, singing, praying for others and longing for the birth of a new soul! Can we turn our sorrow into a song, our despair into a dance by reaching out to one another? Let us cherish the transforming power of love, for we can all join in the song while celebrating the joy of giving and receiving.

Waiting With Hope

THE FOLLOWING PRAYER clearly expresses the way many of us wait: "Dear God, give me the gift of patience and I want it right now!"[5] John's story of God reveals an alternative. On numerous occasions, regardless if it was a major or minor concern, John knew how to wait with hope.

One morning in the corridor of the retirement center, I met John in his wheelchair as the nurse's aide was pushing him. With a friendly hello, John said: **"I was waiting for you! I knew you would come today, but I wasn't expecting to meet you now."** With a laugh, John said: **"You can push me; I'll let you."** As we went down the hall, people just seemed to pop up out of the woodwork and gravitated to John. Staff members and residents, alike, all stopped to talk to him. John seemed to have a kind word, a smile, a listening ear for each person he met. When we were alone, John gently said: **"I'm sick and weak, but people seem to be drawn to me even now. Everyone comes to me looking for something. I can't figure it out. I just try to help people; I just want to love people."** When we are free of repression, tenseness and nervous energy, people are drawn to us like a magnet. When we know how to wait with hope, then we can also remain calm and peaceful.

Another day, John said: **"I'm going to the dance tonight. People tell me: 'You could fall. You could hurt** yourself.' I tell them: 'I'm dying — you know! When you're dying, what is there to be afraid of?' I told someone else: 'I'm not dead, yet! I'm still alive. Tonight, I'm going dancing! Will you join me?' " John went to the party that evening and enjoyed dancing with several of the women. He even performed his traditional tap dancing routine with his cane. When John became tired, he sat down in his wheelchair; however, he still continued to dance by moving his hands, arms and shoulders to the music. Can our spirits soar with such laughter and joy while we wait?

After returning from vacation, I told John about a redwood tree that is 2,700 years old. John laughed and replied: "**I saw it planted when I was a young child. Time's no big deal. Some things are worth waiting for — you know!**" While holding and patting my hand, John said: "**Oh, to have a friend like this — it's worth waiting for — you know!**" While each of us waits, can we too realize: "**Time's no big deal.**"

During an illness, all of life can seem like a continual waiting process. One afternoon, John declared: "**I'm waiting for the doctors to come, and tell me what they are going to do next. I listen to what the doctors say, but I know God is in charge.**" On another morning, John stated: "**I've been waiting to feel stronger, so I can go to church. Last Sunday, I finally felt up to it. My son and I went to mass in the morning. I was so happy just being in church. During the mass, my son said things that made me laugh. He's very funny — you know. Then, all we had to do was just look at each other and we'd laugh. The nuns turned around to see what all the commotion** was about. I thought, 'We're going to get in trouble with the good sisters!' Then, I laughed some more. I don't think God would mind that we were laughing in his house." One day John said: "**I've been waiting for a good meal. Yesterday, my daughter made me pancakes for breakfast and they were wonderful.**"

It is an art to be able to enjoy simple pleasures in the here and now while we wait. One morning, John shared with me: "**I've been waiting to feel better, so I can go outside and get some fresh air.**" In the meantime, John was sitting in the kitchen by the counter and was simply enjoying the view out the window. On another day, John said: "**My son and I went outside today. The warmth of the sun, the sky, the trees, the breeze — it was wonderful. The ducks had their babies.**" I was smiling and delighting in John's spirit of joy. He said: "**Your eyes are so bright and 'sparkley.' I feel like I just want to get in line and absorb their radiant glow.**" John winked at me and asked: "**Do you have a secret to tell me? You look so happy. Is there something you want to tell me? Do you and your husband have some exciting news? Not yet! Well, then, I will simply <u>enjoy waiting</u> for the news.**"

If John could wait with such joy and hope as he was approaching death, surely each of us can wait with a positive disposition — during all the birthing, dying and rebirthing cycles that we experience. Can all of us wait with gratitude? Let us, together, pray:

> *"It is good to give thanks to the LORD,*
> *to sing praise to your name, Most High,*
> *to proclaim your kindness at dawn*

> *and your faithfulness throughout the night,*
> *with ten-stringed instrument and lyre,*
> *with melody upon the harp"* (Psalm 92:2-4).

If we believe in God's imagination, creative energy and divine vision, then we can wait with hope.

The Lord's Servant

"I AM THE LORD'S SERVANT. Each morning, I still put on my suit coat and tie; but I have nowhere to go. Once I sit down, I can't get back up. When someone knocks on my door, by the time I get there the person is gone. I fall asleep when people come to visit, not because they are boring but because I get tired a lot. I may be funny-looking, but I am still the Lord's servant. No matter where I am in life, God wants me — imagine that!" God meets us where we are; however, our challenge is to meet God's acceptance and love with an open, receptive heart. We can be stripped of our career, health and even loved ones; but we can still continue to delight in our "interior gift — our union with God."[6]

"Once I knew a man who was a drunk. His money went to drinking instead of to his family. He wasted away his life drinking. Eventually, his wine became one with the wine of Christ, when one day he drank from the very cup of Christ and was healed." Just as the bread and wine is changed into Jesus, so too, the Eucharist changes each of us. However, the transformation in our lives usually happens gradually over time. God can use even our addictions to unite us to his Greater Power and lead us into service.

"With a little bit of prayer — no, with a lot a bit of prayer — we will all know what we are to do next." Scripture reassures us:

> *"While from behind, a voice shall*
> *sound in your ears:*
> *'This is the way; walk in it' " (Isaiah 30:21).*

"No matter where we are in life, God wants us! We are all the Lord's servants."

Laughter — The Best Medicine

"LAUGHTER IS TRULY GOD'S HAND upon the shoulder of our troubled and hurting world."[7] "Perhaps God is really a comedian playing to an audience that has forgotten how to laugh."[8] Can we live out these words: "Be like a tea kettle, and whistle even when you are up to your neck in boiling hot water."[9]

In the midst of illness and physical pain, John could laugh and talk in a whimsical and playful way:

"I want to go to church to talk to that Guy, Jesus. I would go in my Cadillac" (pointing to wheelchair).

"This morning I wanted to go to work. I feel lazy when I don't go to work. I'm retired, so my work is to rest. It's hard work to rest all day."

"I own this joint, but I can't keep track of who all these people are who keep coming and going in and out of my home. I figure since I own this place, they must all work for me. God forbid they leave me alone; I might jump out the window."

"My wife will be waiting for me at the Gates of Heaven. She will say: 'I always thought you were a pretty smart guy. What took you so long to get here? You're no better than the rest!'"

Even in times of suffering, our grinning God shines through our soul amid all the changing rhythms of life. Rolling, tumbling, journeying along in a whirlwind of laughter and glee – the Father, Son and Holy Spirit radiate new life while embracing each of us through the heartbeat of creation. Can we dance to the drum of life and experience true healing, by joining the Spirit in the telling of tales, singing, laughing and creating?

Riches in Heaven

FEELING ANXIOUS AND ANNOYED, John declared: "I've paid all my bills, so I guess I can die now.

"When I lost my job, or when sales went down, it was rough trying to support my family.

"When my wife and I retired, we sold our home. We had to sell our home before we could afford our new place. It worked out, but what a worry it all was.

"First my wife was sick; now I'm sick. These medical bills and all the paper work are enough to kill you.

"I've given to the Church all my life. I seem to be on the mailing list of every charity organization. Everyone wants my money.

"When I got real sick, my daughter hired a live-in; but I paid for him.

"My daughter does my grocery shopping. She handles all my finances and pays all my bills. She's good at managing things. Sometimes I wonder how much money I have left, so I ask my daughter: 'What's the magic number?' Then I realize...."

John began to laugh and stated: "I've never seen a hearse pull a U-Haul moving truck, but I've heard that in Heaven the pension lasts forever and I believe God's health care plan is the best."

Ah, when one possesses a wealth of wisdom and treasures of love and laughter, then one is truly rich.

God Loves A Humble Heart

LOOKING A BIT PUZZLED, John said: "My son salutes me. I don't know why my son salutes me. I'm just a little guy; I'm not a big guy. I'm weak; I'm not strong.

"I have to do what everyone tells me to do. I'm not the boss; God is the Boss and I try to get on His good side.

"I get into all the wrong things. Sometimes I get angry and mean. I pray: 'Jesus Christ, Our Savior, have mercy on me.'

"This sickness makes me smell bad — it gives my body a bad odor. Now I will go to God just as I am, a little stinker.

"I'm the most confused man, for I always say the wrong thing and make a fool of myself.

"In spite of it all, I'm the luckiest man. I must be near Heaven. This is Heaven. I have family and friends who love me. We have music. God is here."

John's litany reflects the Psalms, for his soul seemed to be singing:

> "My sacrifice, O God, is a contrite spirit;
> a heart contrite and humbled..." (Psalm 51:19).

Oh, God loves a humble heart! St. John of the Cross explains that when we are reduced to nothing and in a state of complete humility, then our soul can unite with

God and our nothingness will be transformed into fire.[10]

85 Years Young

(This essay was written from the point of view of John, but only the sentences in bold print are John's actual words.)

MY EYESIGHT HAS BECOME DIM, but I can still see with my heart.

My hair is as white as snow and my face is wrinkled with age; I hope that is the trademark of years of experience and wisdom, which comes only from living life deeply.

My body is slowing down, but God speaks in quiet stillness and I listen.

My feet and legs can no longer dance, yet my spirits soar into the heavens with leaps and bounds.

Please, do not take me for a fool; I see and move in dimensions that transcend time and space. One minute I see:

"There are six men around my bed and they are smiling at me. I see the faces of so many children; they look so somber. Is it my time?"

"The next minute my son says: 'Dad, I have to give you something that is going to hurt and you will feel such pain. I don't want to hurt you, but then it is going to help you feel better.'"

Could it be, perhaps, that is what death is like as God, Our Father, says: "My Little One, for a while you are going to hurt and feel pain. I don't want you to suffer; but soon you will feel better, soon you will be home with me."

If you would but sit with me, you too could experience the magic — for God is near.

I can turn the ordinary into the extraordinary and transform the mundane into the mystical, for my soul is touching Spirit.

Truly, I am ready to plunge into the next adventure, for

*"Eye has not seen, ear has not heard,
nor has it so much as dawned on man
what God has prepared for those
who love him.
Yet God has revealed this wisdom to
us through the Spirit"* (1 Corinthians 2:9-10).

Oh, to be 85 years young!

The Secret to Success

ONE MORNING when John and I were looking at photographs of times past and going down memory lane, we came across some awards and certificates he had received when he was in sales. John said: "**Everyone thought I made a lot of money. Everyone thought I was successful. It wasn't me; it was God. I was working with God. Along the way, I met other people who were interested in working with God. We joined forces and worked with God together and our business grew. It was wondrous, exciting and fun!**

"Here's the secret to a successful business. Every night I would get down on my knees and pray: 'Lord, I don't have the answer to this problem; but you have all the answers. Please help me! Give me a sign! Tell me what you want me to do!' God always gave me a sign. Often it wasn't the sign I wanted or even expected, but a sign always came. Then I simply acted on the sign because I believed in my heart and soul it was what God wanted me to do.

"Now, everyone thinks I'm retired because I'm not making a lot of money anymore. But, I'm still working with God and I'm really working overtime now! Everyone thinks I'm old and sick; people tell me to rest and that I'm not to do anything! How can you not do anything? Here's what I do! As I lie here in bed, all day long I try to make contact with Jesus Christ in a deep and intimate way. Every person who walks into this room I try to make contact with, in a deep and intimate way. Making contact with God, making contact with people — that is what life is all about. That is what I try to do!

"Now I would like to pass my business on to you! Just remember, as long as you are into the power and glory of God, you are in the right business." John seemed to be leaving me his very heart and soul — what an inheritance, what an investment, what a security trust — to continue the work of Our Father's Business!

"Everything I Have Is Yours!"

DEEP IN THOUGHT, John folded his arms. With a long sigh, he gently said: **"I love my family; I hope they know that! What can I give them? What do they need? I long to ask each of them: 'Is there anything I have that you want? Take it; it's yours! Everything I have is yours. What can I give you?'"** John and his family reveal that love and friendship are the greatest gifts we can give one another.

John's question echoes throughout scripture.

*"The LORD appeared to Solomon in a dream at night.
God said,
'Ask something of me and I will give it to you.'
Solomon answered....
'Give your servant, therefore, an understanding heart...'"*
(1 Kings 3:5,9).

*"Elijah said to Elisha,
'Ask for whatever I may do for you,
before I am taken from you.'
Elisha answered,
'May I receive a double portion of your spirit'"*
(2 Kings 2:9).

John's words of fatherly love resonate in the story of

the Prodigal Son. The elder son holds onto his anger, bitterness and pain unwilling to forgive. He refuses to come to the party, enjoy the music and join in the dancing. He is alone, in the dark, the cold — completely missing the celebration. The father comes to him saying:

> *"You are with me always,*
> *and everything I have is yours"* *(Luke 15:31).*

John's brotherly love reflects Christ's words to his apostles. Before his death, Jesus said:

> *"Peace is my farewell to you,*
> *my peace is my gift to you"* *(John 14:27).*

In the same way, our loved ones who are dying give us the gift of their wisdom, spirit, forgiveness and peace. All we need are eyes that see, ears that hear, an open mind and an accepting heart — to receive, cherish and treasure their gifts. We are yesterday, today and tomorrow; we are forever, because we are held in God's love. Can we enter into this unending love song by waltzing with the Spirit from the Alpha to the Omega? The Spirit proclaims:

> *"See, I make all things new!...*
> *I am...*
> *the Beginning and the End"* *(Revelation 21:5,6).*

To Rest In God

(A Soul Struggling to Die and A Soul Struggling to Live are meant to represent each and every one of us.)

A SOUL STRUGGLING TO DIE:
"HE'S STARING AT ME. That Guy, Jesus, is staring at me. I want Him to smile, but He's just staring at me."

A SOUL STRUGGLING TO LIVE:
"I'm sure it is a loving look."

A SOUL STRUGGLING TO DIE:
"Yes, it is a loving look! The devil's here too. The devil is sitting on my shoulder and I say: 'Go away! Get out of here! Leave me alone.'"

A SOUL STRUGGLING TO LIVE:
"Would you like to pray together?"

A SOUL STRUGGLING TO DIE:
"Why pray for me? I'll be with God soon! Let's pray for you. You're the one who has to keep on living. Soon I'll be leaving. You will be staying. I pray that you will stay as long as you like. May you always hear God laughing, always remember that God is in a hug and may your spirit always dance."

(He gives my hand a kiss, squeezes it, pats it.) **"This**

hand has to stay with me. When you go, this hand stays. I just want to hold it. You've got another one! You don't need two."

(He struggles to stay awake. He keeps opening his eyes to look at me.) **"My tongue is tied. There's so much I want to say to you; but I'm too tired, too weak."**

A SOUL STRUGGLING TO LIVE:
"Good friends can just sit in silence. Words are not needed. Just rest, John, just rest. I'll stay with you."

A SOUL STRUGGLING TO DIE:
Oh, to rest in God. Like a baby resting in the arms of his mother, like an infant's heart resting upon the mother's heart, let me simply rest in God's arms. Let my heart truly rest upon God's heart. Let the deep peace of God cradle and rock my weary body into a sleep that re-creates, renews and restores my restless soul. I long to hear the loving, soothing lullaby of the Life-giving Spirit of God who gently sings the secret of just being.

(Then, eyes closed while resting, with a smile and a wave of the hand, with an expression of joy and ecstasy, with a tone of awe and wonder, he whispers.) **"Do you see it? Do you see it? It's like all the walls have come tumbling down and I can see into all the rooms. I can see everything! I can see everywhere. Do you see it? Oh, you can't see it."** (He pats my hand.)

A SOUL STRUGGLING TO LIVE:
I long to see; I sense that I am standing on Holy Ground, for my friend is encountering the Divine. May

the walls of fear, despair, and negativity that all of us experience come tumbling down, so we too can look at life in a new way.

My Crucifix

"Good morning! It's always a good morning if you are in it. You have a beautiful smile. What time is it? Oh, it's ten o'clock in the morning. It's time to begin a new day — you, God and me.

"God, I see you up there. You're funny. No, erase that (pretends he's using an eraser to clean a blackboard); what I meant to say is you are humorous. I hear you laughing and you are smiling down on us.

"Did you see the crucifix my son gave me? It's right next to my bed. It comes with candles and holy water. Oh, there it is — that pain. I'm very sick. This is my crucifix (holding abdomen in pain)! I think my silence caused my cancer. I always held all my pain inside; I just didn't know what else to do. I still don't know what to do about it. I'll let the Lord take care of it."

> "The LORD binds up the wounds of his people,
> he will heal the bruises..."(Isaiah 30:26).

Can we be open to God's healing grace, so we can forgive and let go of our pain?

"I will die soon. Now I'm just waiting to die."

> "My soul waits for the LORD
> more than watchmen for the morning"
> (Psalm 130:6).[11]

"I don't know what Heaven will be like with everybody up there. I hope I'll go to Heaven; I'm not a saint. But for now, I'm just here."

> *"I give no thought to what lies behind*
> *but push on to what is ahead.*
> *My entire attention is on the finish line*
> *as I run toward the prize to which God calls me —*
> *life on high in Christ Jesus"* (Philippians 3:13-14).

Why Does Our Time Together Have To Be So Short?

"SOON I WILL HAVE TO leave you for God. You know that, don't you? It's only for God that I leave you. Why does our time together have to be so short? Why would God bring an old man and a young woman together for such a short time?

"Am I helping you in some small way? If I'm helping you, then I can't die and leave you; I must stay even if I'm in pain. Still, when the time is right and God calls, what else can I do but go? I want to go to God, but I don't want to leave you. When it is my time, will you come with me? I guess you can't, but I wish you could. I must go; you must stay! Will my family be all right after I'm gone? It's so hard to leave everyone.

"There are six men around my bed; they are all smiling and saying: 'John, come with us.' I told them: 'I have a young woman here with me. Why would I want to go somewhere with six guys, when I have a young woman here with me?' They laughed.

"Our time together is so short, but our love will last forever."

"You have heard me say,
'I go away for a while, and I come back to you'....
I tell you this now, before it takes place,

so that when it takes place you may believe" (John 14:28,29).

God As Trickster

"I can't remember your name. I love you so, and I think about you all the time. I'm always praying for you. It embarrasses me that I can't remember your name."

My soul gently sings: "I give thanks to my God every time I think of you..." (Philippians 1:3), John!

Pointing to his son in the next room, who was the primary caregiver, John shared with me: "I asked him, 'Are you my son or are you my father?' He said: 'Dad, I'm your son, but I've taken on a new role of authority.' I told him: 'If I'm the father, then I should be in charge.' I don't feel like I'm in charge."

Due to the son's constant presence and loving ways, on another day John asked him: "Are you my mother?" The son replied: "If you want me to be." John laughed and thought that was very funny!

On another occasion, John said: "I often make a fool of myself, but people still seem to like me. Imagine that!"

Yet John always knew who God was. One day in a loud booming voice with a twinkle in his eyes, John prayed: "Jesus Christ, Son of God, you're funny. God, you created me. I'm funny-looking, so you must be funny."

Can we recognize that God is the Creator, while we are the mere creature? Can we begin to realize that only

God is perfect and we are not meant to be perfectionists? Can we embrace our humanness by simply accepting that we are incomplete, and acknowledging that only God can make us whole? Can we mess up, look foolish, make mistakes and not have to win all the time? Perhaps it is our imperfections that make each of us so lovable.

The biggest enemy of humor is the need to control. When we want power and want to be in control, then we cannot express feelings and we cannot be vulnerable. Can we turn all power over to God?

Does God use humor to get at our rigidities and pretenses, to loosen up situations and build community? God is forever turning our world upside down, pulling the rug out from under us, shattering our old beliefs about life so we can be open to a new way of being. Is God a bit of a Trickster? How can we dance with a Trickster?

Can we allow the God of Surprises to embrace our total being and sweep us off our feet? Can we dance with Our Maker, gliding right through life's chaos and whirling past contradictions? Only God can bring harmony to all the discords and irregularities of life. The following prayer beautifully expresses the life-giving experience of dancing to God's Plan:

> *"Giver of life, creator of all that is lovely,*
> *Teach me to sing the words to your song;*
> *I want to feel the music of living*
> *And not fear the sad songs*
> *But from them make new songs*
> *Composed of both laughter and tears.*
> *Teach me to dance*

*to the sounds of your world
and your people,
I want to move in rhythm with your plan,
Help me to try to follow your leading
To risk even falling
To rise and keep trying
Because you are leading the dance."*[12]

Dancing In Our Hearts

"I WAS WISHING YOU **would come, and now, here you are."** Pointing to the radio, John said: **"Isn't the music wonderful? Chaplain, please say a prayer for us. If I pray I might mess it up."** Sometimes we do stumble, fall and fail. Even our weaknesses and flaws show what a delightful sense of humor Our Creator has. What a wonderful way to teach us how much we need one another and God.

John asked: **"Do you have any funny stories to share with me? Is there any good news happening in the world today? How are you doing? Are you happy? Anytime you want a hug, I'm always here. You don't even have to ask."**

John told me: **"My first great-grandchild will be born soon! My son said: 'Dad, then you won't be just a grandfather. You will be a great-grandfather.' Imagine that!"**

God is truly present in all the rhythms of birthing, dying and rebirthing. Our Lord is forever dancing in our hearts, encouraging us to join the Great Dance.

> *"There is an appointed time for everything,*
> *and a time for every affair under the heavens.*
> *A time to be born, and a time to die...*
> *A time to weep, and a time to laugh;*
> *a time to mourn, and a time to dance"*
> *(Ecclesiastes 3:1-2,4).*

Live Out the Dream

ONE BRIGHT, SUNSHINY MORNING, John cheerfully announced: "**I enjoy the high school student who visits me. He's a fine young man. We have fun playing checkers together. He doesn't know what he wants to do with his life. I try to help him.**" With a wink of the eye, John laughed and said: "**I help him by beating him at checkers to teach him how to concentrate more. Even though I always win, he keeps coming back every week! He'll be great at whatever he does, because he doesn't ever give up.**" How do we discover our niche in life? How can we each experience life in a deeper and richer way?

When the Holy Spirit and the human spirit embrace and become one, this is the beginning of new life. God's dream is conceived in the human heart, is born in the sparkle of the human eye, touches the human mind and moves within the human will.

The only way that God's will and our will can become one is through quiet stillness. Oh, Spirit of Life, please help us to simply rest with our dream — cherishing it, holding it close to our heart, rocking it back and forth with tenderness and love. Then, our dream will regenerate our restless soul.

Oh, Giver of Hope, empower us to set our dream free; so that it can grow, stretch, play and dance where it will. Our dream has wings and will carry us to new horizons. Can we trust the Guiding Spirit of God's love?

Great love leads to great dreams, but it all starts with small beginnings. Why are we always so impatient, so eager to speed up the unfolding of God's plan? Can we just enjoy the process and simply live out the dream? Then, we can all sing:

*"God who is mighty
has done great things for me" (Luke 1:49).*

Just A Big Kid

"I GUESS I'M AN OLD MAN NOW. My hair and my beard are all white, but I can remember my childhood Christmas like it was yesterday. I can still see the Christmas tree, the colorful lights, all the presents and how the toy train goes round and round.

"As a child, I loved to play baseball. We played a team called Blessed Sacrament. I guess they weren't that blessed: because we beat the pants off Blessed Sacrament! That was some game; we were the champs.

"Then, somehow it happened. I was no longer a child; I was a man. I had my career in sales, fell in love, raised my family, got involved in my community and parish; but I always loved children.

"On family vacations, I had my kids draw a map of where we were going and keep a journal of each day of the trip. I was a Boy Scout leader.

"Years ago when my niece was having a bad day, I lifted her onto my lap and told her a story about a rabbit. I created this special story just for her on the spur of the moment. She still remembers it — imagine that!

"When my kids became teenagers, I taught high school sexuality and religion to all boys. On the first day of class, a freshman said to me: 'So what do you know about sex?' I replied: 'I have one son right here, another son in the next room and two more kids at

home.' " With a twinkle in his eyes, John rubbed his hands together and said: **"I told him, 'Let me tell you what I know about sex.'"** John's humor and wit removed all the barriers of a generation gap, for the doors of communication were opened and any power struggles between adults and teens were thrown to the wind.

John continued: **"As I watched my family grow, I enjoyed gardening. Every day before going to work, I would get up at the crack of dawn to tend the garden. My wife made ketchup with all the tomatoes; however, once in the cellar several bottles exploded. What a mess! I guess life is always full of surprises.**

"I don't know where all the time went. Now I'm an old man, but I still feel like I'm just a big kid." Regardless of our age, we each possess an inner child that frees us to plunge into the dance of life with a carefree spirit. Perhaps, each one of us is **"just a big kid."**

A Weed is the Best

"A WEED IS THE BEST. It's sad that a weed doesn't know it is the best. Everyone is always trying to pull it up and throw it away. People are always trying to kill and destroy it. We always curse at weeds while attempting to get rid of them.

"A weed is a survivor! In the ugliest, most awful environments and against all odds, a weed grows toward the light. It does not grow on its own power; rather, it grows as a result of the power of God. Just as in the evening the sun goes down, so too there are times when God says, 'You don't need my power right now!' Then the weed must wait in darkness. Just as the sun comes up in the morning, so too, when the time is right, God will give the weed the power and grace it needs. All growth comes from God, in God's good time.

"Whenever one sees a weed, one sees God. Wherever weeds are present, God is there. That's why weeds are the best!

"I do not have magical powers. I remember and share these words with the help of God. Now you must remember and share these words with the help of God.

"We need to give thanks for the humble weed within each of us, that truly reveals God's power and glory."

In the Very Heart of God

HAS OUR FAITH JOURNEY ever gone behind a cloud? Has God ever seemed silent? Jesus prayed from the cross:

> *"My God, my God, why have you forsaken me?"*
> (Mark 15:34)

Perhaps, the deepest suffering is feeling abandoned by God. If Jesus had a need to pour out his heartache and pain to God, how much greater our need. Can we — being the weak, frail humans we are — be as honest and real with our faith? Can we share even our pain with God; so that we can work through it and not get stuck in the muck of anger, frustration, fear and negativity? John knew how to work through the pain and transform it with the grace of God.

"I'm very sick! No one knows what to do. You would think someone would know, but no one knows what to do.

"No matter what I eat or drink, nothing tastes good. Everything has gone flat. Every day seems the same.

"I don't know what to do! I'm just here. I'm very sick. I'm not a soldier, but I feel like a war is going on in my body.

"Lord, I was wondering: is it coming to the end of the world? Or is it just coming to the end of me? When

I die, then what happens? Will you be there, God?

"I toss and turn; no position feels comfortable. Oh, there it is again — that pain. Why does it have to hurt so much?

"God, when I fell, I was all alone and I banged myself up. I guess you were busy that day. Where were you? Why didn't you help me?

"Now I'm asking you to help me, to heal me. I have things to do. I want to go to church tomorrow.

"I'm very sick. I don't know what to do. I'm dying; my time is very near. I'm afraid to go to God. It's spinning round and round. I don't want to go on that. I don't like things that spin."

Scripture comforts us with the words:

"...no more will you weep;
he will be gracious to you when you cry out,
as soon as he hears he will answer you.
The Lord will give you the bread you need
and the water for which you thirst" (Isaiah 30:19-20).

"Oh, isn't it time for a hug? When we are together, it is like we are in God — we are in the very heart of God."

Only the eyes of faith can see that even in the midst of suffering, we are in the very heart of God. Let us put all our cares in God's hands, trusting that God cares for us. Then, we can all pray:

"Father, into your hands I commend my spirit"
(Luke 23:46).

I Will Always Be With You

WHEN I WENT TO VISIT John, he said: "**Oh, I was having a terrible day. I prayed to God: 'Jesus Christ, Our Lord and Savior, take me.' But now you are here, so it is a good day. What is between us could only come from God.**

"**God put a little bit of good in me, and every now and then it shoots out so I can pass it on to others. I'm not trying to hold on, I'm just trying to pass on to you. Oh, if I could just be a part of you, forever.**

"**Let's just go to Heaven right now. Why stick around this place? In Heaven, we could find some nice quiet room to be alone.**"

Perhaps John's love gives us a glimpse of what a marvelous lover God is. We are the beloved of God, for we are all precious in the eyes of Our Creator who sings an intimate love song to each of us:

> *"Arise, my beloved, my beautiful one,*
> *and come!*
> *O my dove in the clefts of the rock,*
> *in the secret recesses of the cliff....*
> *How beautiful you are, how pleasing,*
> *my love, my delight"* (Song of Songs 2:13-14,7:7).

This is the greatest love story. God, Our Eternal Lover, is constantly enticed, attracted, excited, allured and drawn to each of us. The Creative Force of God longs to enter into a close union with our whole being. The Enduring Love of God delights in becoming one with all of us. With burning passion and great desire, God is after us. God is forever calling, inviting, reminding and fulfilling.

When it was time for me to leave, John asked when I would return and I replied Monday. He said, **"Monday is a good day; so is Tuesday, Wednesday, Thursday, Friday, Saturday and Sunday. You are welcomed here every day. I love you and I think about you all the time; so even when you are away, you are here."**

Our God of Compassion tenderly whispers to each of us:

*"With an age-old love,
I have loved you"* *(Jeremiah 31:3).*

God's embracing arms reach out and touch our past, present and future with the healing power of unconditional love.

Showers of Love

"WHEN YOU'RE OLD AND SICK, people come in to give you a shower or a bath. It's hard having strangers take your clothes off. They don't ask you if you want a bath or shower. They just say, 'John, you need to have a shower!'" In Heaven, will we still have to take showers?

"I know God has showered me with love. My family is so good to me and I love them all.

"I love you and I love God for allowing me to feel this great love as I am dying. It's such a grace. Other people die and they don't receive this grace. Why do I receive this grace? I don't know; let them figure it out. I've just got the grace because I've got you. I pray that this love will always be good and pure. I can just feel the grace that surrounds you. I love you." St. Teresa of Avila explains that God is the one who "awakens love in the soul."[13]

God has showered all of us with love and blessings:

> "...just as from the heavens the rain
> and snow come down ....
> Yes, in joy you shall depart,
> in peace you shall be brought back;
> Mountains and hills shall break out in song before you,
> and all the trees of the countryside shall clap their hands"
> (Isaiah 55:10,12).

The Tenderness of God

"The nurse's aide washes my face, my teeth, even my butt. The nurse pokes and probes me and says: 'John, I'm going to stick my finger up your rump!' Can you imagine that? I guess there are better things to think about!"

> "O LORD, you have probed me and you know me;
> you know when I sit and when I stand;
> you understand my thoughts from afar"
> (Psalm 139:1-2).

Now, there's something to think about!

"I have my very own chaplain. You come to visit just me. When you are here, it is a holy time, because I believe God put you here. Whether we are together five minutes or two hours, I feel like we are alone with God. When I climb up to Heaven, will you come with me?"

John lovingly reached out his arms to give me a hug and said: **"Oh, this is wonderful — just you and me, and me and you."** While still holding me, John began to look inside and around our embrace, saying: **"We're together and surely God must be here, somewhere. Oh, God is in a hug."**

"Now I'm going to rest. Do you hear the music my son is playing? While I rest, I'm just going to hold your hand, smile and enjoy it. I'm too tired to talk, but I can

still smile."

God, Our Lover, tenderly speaks to each of us with true intimacy:

> *"Set me as a seal on your heart,*
> *as a seal on your arm;*
> *For stern as death is love,*
> *relentless as the nether world is devotion;*
> *its flames are a blazing fire.*
> *Deep waters cannot quench love,*
> *nor floods sweep it away" (Song of Songs 8:6-7).*

Oh, love is a gift freely given, never earned and certainly never deserved. Let us celebrate our humanness, which yearns for the tenderness of God in order to be made whole.

May I Say a Few Words, God?

"I'M JUST A STUPID HUMAN. Lord Jesus Christ, you are a man and you are God. I am just a man; but may I say a few words, God? It's hard to keep up with you. I want to go with you; I want us to go together.

"Now, let me say a few words for you — What's your name again? — MaryAnne, I've been to Heaven and I've seen your girl (looks at me and pats my hand), and she's all ready to come to you. I don't know when God will send her to you. God will be with you. You have the strength.

"There's a spiritual bond between us, and God put it there. I'm very sick. My flesh is dying, but the spiritual bond will always be between us. Do you know what that means?"

I replied, "I know that you will always be a part of me." John said, **"Yes, I will sit with you, walk with you and even ride with you through life."** I continued, "I don't know how that will affect me or what exactly that means."

John responded: **"I don't know what it means either. Only God knows. Dear God, we are only humans and we can't remember or understand these things. Let us just enjoy this spiritual bond today.**

"God, you placed this attraction between us. Please give priests, brothers, nuns and teachers more attraction so people will listen to their message. Kids in high school need to feel this attraction towards their teachers. The attraction between people comes from you, God. You have to help us.

"I used to read from the Book and sing during Sunday liturgies. Then I became sick and they said, 'John, you can't read or sing anymore.' I felt bad; I had done this all my life."

I replied, "John, now you speak and sing words that come straight from your heart and soul. You are sharing your own stories of God all the time."

John laughed and said, **"You have a way with words and you always say the right thing. You can make sense out of the babbling of an old man."**

"Be Near Me"

(This essay was written from the point of view of John, but only the sentences in bold print are John's actual words.)

When I am too tired to talk and there is nothing to say, for words seem meaningless:
"JUST BE NEAR ME!"
When I am too weak to hold your hand or even give a hug, don't be afraid to touch me. You can still hug and hold me for I will always feel love, gentleness and tenderness. Even **"my son's little dog knows how to snuggle up to me;"** so,
"JUST BE NEAR ME!"
When all I do is sleep and when I never seem to be alert or coherent, you can still talk to me, for I hear everything you say. You can tell me that you love me, that you will miss me, but reassure me that it is time to return home and let me know that you will be fine when I leave. Send me from your loving embrace to God's loving embrace; so,
"JUST BE NEAR ME!"
When I open my eyes, your loving look and gentle touch speak volumes. When I see my tears in your eyes, I know I am not alone. Truly, all that is beautiful and wonderful in life is felt in the heart; so,
"JUST BE NEAR ME!"

The Gathering

ARE THERE HEAVENLY courts of angels and saints before the throne of God? Or are these merely images and archetypes which resonate deep within our psyche? Do people who are dying truly see visions? Or are these visions merely hallucinations, due to medication and lack of food? I will allow you to reach your own conclusions; let me simply write John's words. Any Scripture passages you read are inserted by me and were not referred to by John. My belief is that whatever John saw, only God and he know; but my friend was experiencing the presence of the Divine in a very powerful and intimate way. As St. Teresa of Avila explains, we need to look at all of life through the "eyes of the soul."[14]

> "See, I am sending an angel before you,
> to guard you on the way
> and bring you to the place I have prepared"
> (Exodus 23:20).

When I walked into the room, John's whole face lit up with a smile and he reached out his arms to give me a warm embrace. After a friendly hello, a kiss and a loving hug, John joyfully said: **"Oh, God is with us!"**

Then, John began to look on either side of his bed, in front of his bed and above him saying: **"You are all important. You are all of worth and value. We are going** to hold a very important meeting. Each of you come forward and announce your name." While I wondered what John was seeing, he lovingly greeted each one with a nod of the head and a smile, with sparkling and radiant eyes. His face became so animated and filled with awe; he seemed to be enjoying the diversity, beauty and wonder of each one. He was spellbound by the magic of the moment, and I chose not to interrupt by asking questions.

After John received the introductions and I was left simply to imagine whom he had greeted, he said: "**Now it is time for us to meditate on the power and glory of God.**" He appeared to be leading his heavenly, angelic friends in a hypnosis exercise of "**self-control**" and "**self-suggestion.**" He seemed to be experiencing an altered state of consciousness as he explained: "**Close your eyes, breathe deeply, center yourself in the very heart of God.**"

John said: "**Before we proceed with our meeting, do we have someone to take the minutes?**" John looked at me and said: "**Did you say you will take the minutes? You must remember, record and write down all that is said. You will then give the report at our next meeting. I know you will do a beautiful job; God will help you remember.**" Looking around at everyone in the room, John said: "**She likes to write, you know!**" John smiled warmly at me and lovingly kissed my hand. "**You don't have to write it now; God will help you put it all together.**"

John continued: "**This is a very important meeting, but we are only one group. We need to get Catholics to begin meeting in small groups. How can we do that? How can we get Catholics more involved? Please, one at** a time, please raise hands. That's a good point. Yes!" John glanced at his watch and said: "**We have to keep this moving along. We don't have a lot of time.**" John turned to me and asked, "**Did you get all that?**" I replied, "Why don't you sum it up for me." John explained: "**They said Catholics have to start meeting in each other's homes.**"

John continued to talk to the assembly and said: "**I will volunteer to have another group meet in my home. All of you have to help new groups of Catholics organize and begin to meet in each other's homes.**"

John asked: "**Does anyone here have a calendar? When should we meet next? Let's say the 55th day of the month on a Wednesday and a Friday.**" John turned to me and said: "**You will present the minutes and give the report at the next meeting.**"

While looking at one corner of the room, John prayed: "**Dear God, I will not be on earth much longer. Come to my home and bring your friends. We have plenty of food. You can help yourself to some coffee. Dear God, I am asking you and your friends to come to my home so that I can begin to feel at home with you, and then one day I will be ready to go to your home. I hear you have a wonderful meal prepared, a true feast waiting for me. Forgive me, God, but I am feeling a bit afraid to come to you. God, please give me the grace I need so that I can come to you.**"

John declared: "**That's all! The meeting is adjourned.**"

John turned to me, rolled over on his side, gave me a wink along with a smile and said: "**They are all gone, but they will be back. It's just you and me, now! It's just us!**"

> *"Do not let your hearts be troubled.*
> *Have faith in God*
> *and faith in me.*
> *In my Father's house there are many dwelling places;*
> *otherwise, how could I have told you*
> *that I was going to prepare a place*
> *for you?*
> *I am indeed going to prepare a place*
> *for you,*
> *and then I shall come back to take*
> *you with me,*
> *that where I am you also may be"* (John 14:1-3).

Can we each have a vision of humanity and divinity being at home with one another? Can our vision reveal values which empower us to build up the Body of Christ? Can we listen to our human spirit to find the Holy Spirit? The Holy Spirit laughs and dances within the dwelling place of the human spirit. That is why dying does not have to be a downer; even death can be upbeat.

The Path to God

WHENEVER WE SEE A CRUCIFIX, can we hear Jesus whisper to each of us: "You are precious in my eyes and I love you!" While John was hugging me, holding me close, he whispered in my ear: **"I love you through Jesus Christ. This is how Jesus Christ loves you. He created you, so he loves you forever and ever. He will never pull away from you."**

> *"I am certain that neither death nor life,*
> *neither angels nor principalities,*
> *neither the present nor the future,*
> *nor powers,*
> *neither height nor depth nor any other creature,*
> *will be able to separate us from the love of God*
> *that comes to us in Christ Jesus, our Lord"*
> *(Romans 8:38-39).*

John said: **"This is the way Jesus Christ loves everyone. All he wants is for us to love him and one another."**

As Scripture reveals:
"No longer will your Teacher hide himself,
but with your own eyes you shall see your Teacher"
(Isaiah 30:20).

John continued: **"I love you so! You have your man.**

You have your God. What do you need me for? Yet I have tried to show you so many things; I've tried to show you the path to God." Our journey of faith is continually ongoing. John asked: **"Will you find your way?"**

> Jesus said:
> *"I am the way, and the truth, and the life;*
> *no one comes to the Father but through me.*
> *If you really knew me, you would know my*
> *Father also"* (John 14:6-7).
>
> *"No one has ever seen God.*
> *Yet if we love one another*
> *God dwells in us,*
> *and his love is brought to perfection in us....*
> *We have come to know and to believe*
> *in the love God has for us.*
> *God is love,*
> *and he who abides in love*
> *abides in God,*
> *and God in him"* (1 John 4:12,16).

The Power of Prayer

DURING MANY OF THE VISITS, John would constantly alternate between resting, praying and talking. While resting, he would breathe deeply with his mouth opened. Then he would pray silently with eyes gazing towards the heavens, smiling and radiating joy. Next, he would speak a few words. This was the pattern: rest some, pray a bit, then talk a while. These visits became peaceful, grace-filled moments, because Our God — "The One Whose Heart Watches Even When He Sleeps" (Song of Songs 5:2)[15] — was revealed to me.

As John was resting with his eyes closed, I would pray silently. Often, my mind would wander. It fascinated me that whatever I longed for, whatever my heart ached for, whatever thoughts came to mind, *John would open his eyes and directly respond to each unspoken wish and each unspoken desire,* regardless if it was significant or insignificant. It was as if he could see through all the clutter, look right into my soul and read my life story like a book. Let us marvel at the All-knowing Spirit of God moving through each of us.

> "*My journeys and my rest you scrutinize,
> with all my ways you are familiar.
> Even before a word is on my tongue,
> behold, O LORD, you know the whole of it*"
> (Psalm 139:3-4).

One day as John was resting with his eyes closed, *I thought silently*: "John, you've been like a loving father. You've given me a glimpse of what a wondrous lover God the Father is." John opened his eyes and gave me a warm, loving smile. We visited for a few minutes just small talk; then John turned to me saying, **"Did you call me father?"** (I had not spoken these words or made any reference to a father.) He threw his head back and roared with laughter. John prayed: **"Dear God, I feel like I've always known this young woman and I just want to be a part of her forever."**

> *"Live on in me, as I do in you ....*
> *As the Father has loved me,*
> *so I have loved you" (John 15:4,9).*

On another occasion, I noticed that John was wearing only a short sleeve shirt and shorts. He was resting with his eyes closed. Seeing his arms and legs, *I thought silently*: "He is a skeleton of skin and bones, for his body is wasting away." With *his eyes still closed*, John said: **"It is not a waste. God is very present to me and God is also present to you. God is here."**

> *"If I go up to the heavens, you are there;*
> *if I sink to the nether world, you are present there....*
> *If I say, 'Surely the darkness shall hide me,*
> *and night shall be my light' —*
> *For you darkness itself is not dark,*
> *and night shines as the day.*
> *(Darkness and light are the same.)"*
> *(Psalm 139:8,11-12)*

On one instance, after returning from a funeral Mass of an elderly woman who had been adopted, I sat with John as he was resting. *I began to reflect* on this woman's life and *wondered silently* if I should adopt a child. John opened his eyes and announced: **"We have to get ready for the baby you are going to have. The baby that you and your husband are going to have. Have you decided on any names?"** John pointed to the heavens, laughed and said: **"Do you see her? She's calling your name. She's a wild one!"**

> "Abram said,
> 'O LORD GOD, what good will your gifts be,
> if I keep on being childless....
> See, you have given me no offspring,
> and so one of my servants will be my heir.'
> Then the word of the LORD came to him:
> 'No, that one shall not be your heir;
> your own issue shall be your heir'....
> Abram put his faith in the LORD"
> (Genesis 15:2-4, 6).

During one visit as John was resting, *I prayed silently*: "God, what is the next step for me? What do you want me to do?" With eyes still closed, John said: **"If you keep on praying, you will know what you are to do next."** Let us sing praise to the Ever-lasting Love of God. We need to celebrate how the Spirit of Our Creator is forever guiding us and giving direction to our life.

"Then you shall call, and the LORD will answer,

> you shall cry for help, and he will say: Here I am!...
> Then the LORD will guide you always"
> (Isaiah 58:9,11).

When John saw that I was surprised and excited that he could directly respond to my unspoken thoughts, he would pat my hand and say: **"God knows what is in your heart. God tells me what is in your heart. I have no special powers."** We were truly united by the Spirit. Perhaps these stories reveal the power of prayer for when we rest in God and become quiet and still, then the Lifegiving Spirit can speak.

> "Be still, and know that
> I am God" (Psalm 46:10, KJV).[16]

When John was near death, he could not talk much. In a very weak voice, straining, laboring and struggling to form slowly each word, John whispered: **"What we are experiencing is very powerful. We have to be very careful. We are not God. God is working through us. We are not doing it; God is! We have to be very careful. We have to always remember that God is simply working through us."**

> "The words I speak are not spoken of myself;
> it is the Father who lives in me accomplishing his works" (John 14:10).

As John was dying, he was so childlike, simple and humble, stripped of all pride and ego for he was completely selfless. As John was approaching death, he was totally trusting and surrendering to God's will. These wondrous qualities were reflected throughout his entire life, bringing a bit of heaven to all he met. Imagine what our world would be like if we could all live in such a state by constantly tapping into the power of God through the power of prayer.

Concerning the power of prayer, St. Teresa of Avila writes: "Wherever God is, there is heaven....Where His Majesty is present, all glory is present....There is no need to go to heaven in order to speak with one's Eternal Father or find delight in Him. Nor is there any need to shout. However softly we speak, He is near enough to hear us. Neither is there any need for wings to go to find Him. All one need do is go into solitude and look at Him within oneself, and not turn away from so good a Guest but with great humility speak to Him as to a father."[17]

God of Celebrations

ONE AFTERNOON, John's son greeted me at the door with the words: "Dad's trying to solve all the problems of the decades. I hope he gets it all sorted out, soon!" It was Friday, four days before John died, and he began to dwell on all the parties, fund raisers and dances he had organized in the past. He was very anxious about the lists and all the details.

John asked his daughter, **"Have you checked the lists for the party? Oh, dear! Is everything ready?"**

His son walked into the room and said, "Did I hear someone say something about a party?" John laughed!

His daughter replied: "Yes, Dad, you did plan lots of parties and dances — all the fund raisers to have our church built, for the Boy Scouts, and for the Knights of Columbus."

Later John shared with me: **"We have to help people who are dying; the temptation is so great."** Feelings of despair, doubting God's existence, wondering if death will result in nothingness — these fears can suddenly become very real to a dying person. Even an individual who has been aware of God's presence, throughout all of life, can experience this inner struggle and turmoil when confronted with the painful reality of one's own death. John pleaded: **"We have to pray for those who are dying. We have to help teenagers. We need more priests. Oh, dear! I don't know what to do! Can you help in some way?"**

Truly, when unexplainable laws of nature bring us trials and tribulations, God gives us our families and friends. Let us flow with the dance of love, death and life — for in the loving is the dying, and in the dying is the rising to new life. Our God of Celebrations has planned a party that is everlasting and we are all invited.

I Will See You — Soon!

THE AUTHOR OF LIFE can transform our tale of trivia into a touching love story. Through John's words a heartwarming, delightful and inspiring story of God is creatively revealed.

Monday afternoon, John was at the threshold of death. He was very weak, very sick. He could not move much; he could not talk much. His daughter and I sat with him for quite a while. As I held John's hand, I felt that there were no more words that needed to be said, no more prayers that needed to be spoken — for his life had become a living prayer. I simply said: "Good-bye, John. I will see you <u>soon</u>! I <u>will see</u> you soon!" Suddenly, very unexpectedly, John's face broke into a beaming, radiant smile and his eyes sparkled; but only for a moment, and then the smile faded. However, the warmth and love of that smile will be with me forever.

> "In a little while the world <u>will see</u> me no more,
> but you <u>will see</u> me;
> and because I live, you also will live.
> When that day comes, you will know
> that I am in my Father
> and that you are in me, just as I am in you"
> (John 14:19-20).[18]

I hear John in the laughter and playfulness of children.
I see him in affectionate, passionate young lovers.

I smell his presence in the aroma of a garden of flowers opening and unfolding to the sun, always remembering that: **"A weed is the best."**

I can almost taste his memory in a sip of Ensure, remembering his words: **"Would you like a drink of Ensure? It's great stuff. Actually, it's awful; but if you drink it, they will think I finished it. We don't ever have to tell them."**

I feel him in the rhythm and heartbeat of music, singing, clapping, cheering and dancing.

I touch John in a hug, a kiss, a squeeze of the hand, a loving look, and a kind word.

I experience John's presence in Scripture and in prayer, through the healing and renewing power of simply resting in God.

John will be with me whenever I encounter the Life-giving Spirit of Our Creator. John has become a guiding force of love and truth, giving direction, strength and joy to my life. "Perhaps death is the greatest cosmic joke of all. Like a child playing peek-a-boo, like a jack-in-the-box, what we thought was gone is present and right in our midst, what we thought was dead is alive in a new and deeper way."* Those of us who believe in the Spirit of Love never meet for the last time. Even death cannot separate us from our loved ones. Oh, let us celebrate all the creative ways God can transform our lives!

*Used with permission.

Dad's In Heaven

TUESDAY MORNING, I felt John had died during the night. I did not want to receive the news over the phone, so I decided to go to his home. John's son answered the door, looked down and said sadly: "Dad's not here. Dad's in heaven. We were all with him; we didn't get much sleep. His great-granddaughter was born yesterday at 3:00 pm. Dad died early in the morning between 1:00 and 2:00 am. We made all the funeral arrangements. For some reason, I woke up early at 6:00 am and washed Dad's linen from his bed. There was a line to use the washing machine even at that hour. I put the linen in the dryer, folded it and thought: 'Dad's not here. Dad's in heaven.'" Perhaps it is in the midst of simple, ordinary and routine tasks that the reality of death slowly sinks in and penetrates us at the core of our being.

> *"Very early,*
> *just after sunrise,*
> *on the first day of the week*
> *they came to the tomb....*
> *they found that the stone had been rolled back.*
> *On entering the tomb*
> *they saw a young man sitting at the right,*
> *dressed in a white robe.*
> *This frightened them thoroughly,*
> *but he reassured them:*

> *'You need not be amazed!...*
> *He has been raised up; he is not here'* "
> *(Mark 16:2, 4-6).*

When a loved one dies, we too can be entombed in grief, pain, guilt, fear or disillusionment; but God rolls away the rock and sets us free. Throughout the suffering, God sends many earthly "angels" who help all of us rise to a new resurrected life that never, ever dies.

The healing journey is a long, slow process in a desert of time. "Loneliness in the absence of the beloved is part of the price we pay for the joys of loving."[19] However, even in the void, the emptiness, the Spirit of Hope dances amid the confusion — empowering us to re-create ourselves and one another. As partners with God, can we trust that from the turmoil and brokenhearted pain comes new beginnings?

On Wednesday afternoon, I went to John's home and visited with his sons and daughter. We began to look through picture albums of John. It was delightful to see all the pictures and hear all the stories. Oh, it is in the remembering and the telling of the stories that a loved one who has died will always be alive and in our midst. Let us rejoice in the bonfire of our human experience, touching Spirit all the while!

The Spirit Continues to Dance

FOUR MONTHS AFTER JOHN'S DEATH, I returned to the grotto of our Lady of Lourdes where John had prayed to the Blessed Virgin, Mother of God, asking that she send someone to comfort him while he was dying. The grotto is located on the grounds of the retirement center where John lived. When I arrived, there was an elderly man about John's age praying before the statue of Mary. He gazed into the face of Our Lady and prayed silently just as John had often done. It was a cold, wintry morning. The wind was still; all was calm and peaceful. The man was absorbed in prayer — communing heart to heart. I could only wonder what needs, hopes, dreams, longings and petitions were in this person's soul.

At the sound of my footsteps, the man turned, greeted me with a warm smile and a friendly wave of the hand. Even though I had never met him before, he immediately began visiting with me and said: "Each morning, I come here to see my Mom. Mary's my Mom you know. Each evening, I go to the chapel to see my Dad. God's my Dad you know. My father always said: 'You have to start and end each day with God and nothing else is important.' "

During another day at the retirement center, I was in the hall behind this same elderly man who was visiting with a nun. Walking slowly with a cane, he announced to the sister: "I went to see my Mom today!" The nun stopped dead in her tracks and said in surprise: "Your mother?" She looked puzzled, wondering if it was possible for a man in his eighties to still have a mother who could be living. The man said, "Yep" and pointed in the direction of the grotto. The sister laughed and said: "Oh, you mean Mary, the Blessed Virgin." He nodded his head and grinned. The man continued: "By the way, sister, are you going to the party tomorrow night? Bring your dancing shoes." The sister replied: "I'm going to the party, but I don't know if I have any dancing shoes." The elderly man declared: "If you want to dance with me, put on your red dancing shoes."

As they giggled like a couple of 14-year olds, I realized that the Spirit I had so loved in John was alive in others as well. I heard God laughing, for it was the same Playful Spirit continuing to dance in their souls. The Spirit is forever tickling the places where we are stiff and rigid, so we can enter into the celebration.

On another occasion, I visited with a woman in her eighties. With a sparkle in her eyes, she said: "When I was your age, I used to love to dance. It's good to be young." This woman is still young in Spirit. Even though she has great difficulty walking with her cane, her dancing days are not over — for she is so full of life and love. While knitting baby bonnets and blankets for the poor and families in need, her fingers seem to dance across her creations — even glide with pure grace and charm. Bent over her labors of love, she simply declared: "While knitting, I pray and feel very close to God."

Our Creator is woven into the very fabric of life, knitted into every fiber of our existence. St. John of the Cross explains that when we unite our soul with Our

Beloved and become one with the will of God, what an intricate pattern and life-giving tapestry is created. In this union of love with God, John states that we begin to love here and now with the cleansing fire of God's unconditional love.[20]

St. John of the Cross gives a vivid image of God and the soul lovingly becoming one. He writes: "And she does not say I alone shall weave the garlands, or you alone will, but we shall weave them together. The soul cannot practice or acquire the virtues without the help of God, nor does God effect them alone in the soul without her help."[21] Can we knit our heart, soul and body to God and plunge into the dance of transformation? Oh, what a delight — to dance through life arm in arm with Our Maker, filled with the Spirit of Wonder.

Join in the Dance of Compassion

ON ANOTHER OCCASION after John's death, I went to visit some of his friends who had long since left the retirement center and are now in a nursing home. As I walked down the corridor, there was no music; the dancing had truly stopped. Many of the elderly were sitting in wheelchairs with a blank, life-less stare looking very sad and lonely.

The words of our elders touch our hearts urging us to become partners in the unending dance. One woman reached out, grabbed my hand, and held on tightly while saying: "Dear, give me a kiss. Just give me a kiss!" Another woman was constantly crying and moaning, when I walked into her room she pleaded: "Take me home. Can't you take me home?" Nearby, a man mumbled: "I'm lost." His wife walked over to hold his hand, and he said to her: "I'm lost without you. Stay with me."

Sooner or later, we will each be old, sick, weak. Regardless of our age or health, we are all in need of mercy, love and understanding. What can we do now? What action can we take right within our own families and communities? As we begin to reach out to our elders, what a life-giving, enriching and nurturing experience it is for us — to encounter those who have lived long enough to discover their true self, their Christ Self. Concerning the talent show John was in, he once said:

"Some people thought I was just a silly, old man wandering around up there, but I was really dancing and I can teach you to dance too!"

The same Playful Spirit of Wisdom that waltzed with Yahweh in the beginning, breathing new life and vitality, is still alive. We are all called and sent to become partners with God and join in the dance of compassion, just as in the beginning. Can we spin, twirl and leap with Our Maker from the dawn to the evening of life? Can we dance hand in hand with one another in a Spirit of love and together embrace the darkness, thereby generating new light?

The Ageless Dance of Love

THE AGE-OLD MELODY of love flows throughout all of life. The past, present and future become one as we celebrate the Word. Whenever we gather for the breaking of the bread, the priest proclaims: "Remember, Lord, those who have died and have gone before us marked with the sign of faith, especially those for whom we now pray.... May these, and all who sleep in Christ, find in your presence light, happiness and peace."[22]

One morning, I went to mass at a chapel dedicated to St. Therese of the Child Jesus. During the Eucharistic prayer, I was remembering John's spirit of love and joy. Suddenly, a three year old child turned to his mother, raised his arms and said: "I want to go up. I want to see Jesus. I want to see Jesus close up." His mother smiled, bent down, lovingly lifted her son and held him in her arms. With eyes of wonder, the child gazed at the cross, the altar and the Eucharist. He looked into the eyes of the priest, the congregation and listened intently to the Word, the music — seeing Christ everywhere. During the consecration when the host was raised, the child excitedly exclaimed: "That's Jesus!"

When it was time to receive communion, the child with his sincere and spontaneous nature wanted to simply run up to the priest in sheer joy. The mother held her son explaining: "We have to wait our turn, we have to go one row at a time." The child started to pull his mother's hand declaring: "I want to go to Jesus! Don't you want to go to Jesus? I want to just be with Jesus!" When they finally reached the priest, the child was in his mother's arms. As the priest said: "Body of Christ," the child gazed intently at the Eucharist, looked down as the host was placed in his mother's hands and watched as she placed "Jesus" in her mouth. With a huge grin the child looked at the priest as if to say: "Isn't this just great!" The priest gently made the sign of the cross on the boy's forehead at which point he shyly buried his face in his mother's shoulder. As they walked back to their seats, the child asked: "Was that Jesus?" Then struggling to distinguish whether the priest or the host was Jesus, he asked: "Was the big one Jesus, or was the little one Jesus?"

Once mass was over, the child was beaming as he said: "Mom, I saw Jesus today." He then began to clap his hands and dance in the aisle. Many people came over to greet the boy, for his presence made it such a joyful celebration. One elderly woman lovingly said: "I see Jesus in you, Dear."

Can we see Jesus in one another and dance with this same Spirit of Ageless Love? Do we encounter Christ in the Word, the Eucharist, and the music? Perhaps that is why John would often ask: **"Did you go to mass today? What were the readings about? What did Jesus say to you? I couldn't go to mass, but Jesus speaks to me right here!"** In the same way, it seemed as if I was "seeing Jesus close up" through John. Now, in a more intimate way than ever before, I experience Christ's presence in the Word, the Eucharist, and the music. What a celebration!

Epilogue
What Can a Dying Person Give?

A warm smile,
A hand to hold,
A listening ear,
Heartfelt hugs,
Inspiration and dreams,
Life-giving prayers,
A loving look that proclaims: "You are precious!"
A spirit that speaks,
A soul that shines,
A wealth of stories,
Songs sung with gusto,
Strength that empowers,
Loyal, encouraging cheers that uplift others!
Life often flies
Like a fast-paced jig,
Whirling quickly by;
But
A dying person
Slows us down,
We become quiet, still,
Returning to our center, our inner core!

EPILOGUE
WHAT CAN A DYING PERSON GIVE

Move with the seasons of life,
    Embrace the changing cycles,
        Celebrate birth, death and rebirth!
Waltz right through the darkness of suffering,
Turn a sad, tragic story into a rainbow of hope and glory,
Oh, whenever there's rhythm, we're dancing with God!

        MaryAnne McCrickard Benas

Grand Finale
The Eternal Shuffle

The Divine Presence leaps, twirls and spins among
the clouds of white,
While roars of laughter explode into brilliant,
dazzling, glowing sunlight.

Grace sings with the birds and connects the heavens
to the earth,
As dancing eyes and heartwarming smiles reveal
true inner worth.

The Sacred slides down rainbows, dances with
the stars, and lassoes the moon.
Oh, all of life is a delightful playground, so let's
joyfully waltz to a new tune.

A Sunny Soul rolls, tumbles, journeys along —
as the Lord's sidekick,
Like two flames dancing and becoming one —
from a slow, steady wick.

The Spirit of Wisdom guides us in the midst of
each and every plight,
Uniting our heart and soul to God's everlasting glory
and great might.

GRAND FINALE
THE ETERNAL SHUFFLE

As Creator and partner dance the tango —
directions shift.
A gliding gait, a playful dip gladly leads to a —
fun loving lift.

Let's join in the eternal shuffle —
the oldest angelic dance step,
While singing: "Live on in my love"*—
and move with new pep.

MaryAnne McCrickard Benas

*(The scripture quote used above is from John 15:9)

Notes

1. <u>The Holy Bible: Today's English Version</u> (New York: American Bible Society, 1992), p. 437.

2. Anonymous.

3. Sue Woodruff, <u>Meditations with Mechtild of Magdeburg</u> (Sante Fe, N.M.: Bear and Co., 1982), p. 47.

4. <u>God on the Dock</u> (Insight Film), Paulist Production, written by Reverend Ellwood Kieser.

5. Anonymous.

6. Steven Payne, O.C.D., <u>Carmelite Studies VI: John of the Cross</u> (Washington D.C.: ICS Publications, 1992), p. 155.

7. Anonymous.

8. <u>Oh God</u> (film), Warner Brothers Communications Company, produced by Jerry Weintraub, directed by Carl Reiner, based on the novel by Avery Corman.

9. Anonymous.

10. Quoted in Payne, <u>Carmelite Studies VI: John of the Cross</u>, p.103 (paraphrased).

11. Revised Standard Version of the Bible (U.S.A.: Division of Christian Education of the National Council of the Churches of Christ, 1971).

12. Anonymous.

13. Quoted in Tessa Bielecki, Teresa of Avila Mystical Writings (New York: Crossroad, 1994), p.137.

14. Ibid., p. 169.

15. Quoted in John Clarke, O.C.D., Story of A Soul the Autobiography of St. Therese of Lisieux (Washington D.C.: ICS Publications, 1972), p.142.

16. The Holy Bible: King James Version (New York: 1st Ballantine Books, 1991).

17. Quoted in Bielecki, Teresa of Avila Mystical Writings, pp. 41-42.

18. The Holy Bible: Today's English Version, p. 1033.

19. Bielecki, Teresa of Avila Mystical Writings, p. 52.

20. Quoted in Payne, Carmelite Studies VI: John of the Cross, pp.148-149 (paraphrased).

21. Ibid., p.145.

22. John J. Limb, <u>Today's Missal Advent/Ordinary Time 1995-1996</u> (Portland: Oregon Catholic Press, 1995), p.83.

Title Description of Books by CMJ Marian Publishers

Lost in the World: Found in Christ By Father Christopher Scadron

The story of a priest ordained at the age of 63 — As a young Jewish man Padre Pio predicated he would become a Priest. After years of floundering and sin as a naval officer and an artist, this unusually gifted and interesting man became a priest at 63! A tale all Catholics will find moving and deeply inspiring, it is also a must gift for any man you know who might be called to the Priesthood at an age older than the usual. $12.50

Becoming the Handmaid of the Lord By Dr. Ronda Chervin

The journals of this well known Catholic writer span her family life as wife and mother, mystical graces sustaining her through a mid-life crisis, the suicide of her beloved son, her widowhood and finally a Religious Sister at the age of 58. Insightful, inspiring & challenging. 327 pages of the heart. $13.75

Ties that Bind By Ronda Chervin

The story of a Marriage. This beautiful novel presents the wife's point of view and the husbands point of view on the same conflict. The author Dr. Chervin has written many books on Catholic life. *Ties that Bind* is both funny and inspiring. A great gift for couples thinking about marriage as well. $ 8.50

The Cheese Stands Alone By David Craig

(The formost religious poet of the day) A dynamite account of a radical conversion from the world of drugs to the search for holiness in the Catholic Church. Realism & poetic imagery combine to make this a must for those who want the real thing. Its a rare book that is both monastic and charismatic — anyone acquainted with the latter will love the chapter on misguided zeal, aptly titled "Busbey Burkeley." $12.50

The History of Eucharistic Adoration By Father John Hardon, S.j.

In an age of widespread confusion and disbelief, this document offers unprecedented clarity in the most important element of our faith. I recommend that it be prayerfully studied and widely circulated. It is thoroughly researched and well documented, and promises to enlighten, instruct and inspire countless souls to an undying love of our Eucharistic Lord. $ 4.00

The Bishop Sheen We Knew By Father Albert Mary Shamon

A booklet filled with little known information from his Vicar, Fr. Albert J.M. Shamon, Bishop Dennis Hickey and Fr. Mike Hogan, the three remaining priests who worked under Bishop Sheen. A chance to see the day to day workings of the acknowledged prophet of our times. $ 4.00

Many new & exciting releases

(If you are interested in any or all of these exciting new titles send us your name and address and we can send you a notice of publication with the price.)

By Way of the Cross By Carol J. Ross

Autobiography. When you read *By Way of the Cross* you will open yourself to tears of empathy and of joy as you see this woman struggling with terribly physical and mental crosses, scooped up into breathtaking visions of the supernatural world.
Paperback. Full color photos. 468 pages. $12.25

Behold the Man, Simon of Cyrene By Father Martin DePorres

Inspired writing by a gifted new Author. This story shows us the gifts given to Simon, through carrying the Cross with Jesus. Simon shares with us the gifts we can expect by carrying our daily crosses. $12.25

Dancing with God through the Evening of Life
By Mary Anne McCrickard Benas

Unique insight into the world of the hospice worker and the patient relationship. The beautiful faithful outlook of a elderly man dying and the gifts he gives us through this experience. $12.75

The Third Millennium Women By Patricia Hershwitzky

Consider the sinking feeling many Catholics get when they see literature about preparing for this great event. They expect what they read or pretend to read to be true, but dull as dishwater. By contrast — here is a book that is wildly funny and also profound. Written by a "revert" (born Catholic who left and then returned), it is also ideal as a gift for those many women we know are teetering on the verge of returning Home.

Messages to the World from the Mother of God

Daily meditative pocketsize prayer book on the monthly messages given the visionaries in Medjugorji for the conversion of the World, back to her son Jesus. These messages for the World started in 1984 till the present. In 1987 the messages began on the 25th of the month (union of two hearts with the 5 wounds of Jesus) thus the 25th. These are from St. James Church in Medjugorji. Great Gift!!! $11.50

Children of the Breath By Martin Chervin

Who would have dared to challenge Creation if, at the close of each new day, God said, "It is perfect." Instead, His lips spoke "It is good. . ." and the serpent was already in Eden. Thus begins *Children of the Breath*, a startling journey into the desert where Christ was tempted for forty days of darkness and light. With immense clarity, lyricism, and humor, author Martin Chervin has delivered a powerhouse that will engage readers of any faith.

To order additional copies of this book:

Please complete the form below and send for each copy

CMJ Marian Publishers
P.O. Box 661 • Oak Lawn, IL 60454
call 708-636-2995 or fax 708-636-2855
email jwby@aol.com

Name _____

Address _____

City _____ State _____ Zip _____

Phone (____) _____

	PRICE EA.	QUAN.	SUBTOTAL
Lost in the World	$12.50 x	____	= $ _____
Becoming the Handmaid of the Lord	$13.75 x	____	= $ _____
Ties that Bind	$ 8.50 x	____	= $ _____
The Cheese Stands Alone	$12.50 x	____	= $ _____
The History of Eucharistic Adoration	$ 4.00 x	____	= $ _____
The Bishop Sheen We Knew	$ 4.00 x	____	= $ _____
By Way of the Cross	$12.25 x	____	= $ _____
Behold the Man!	$12.25 x	____	= $ _____
Dancing with God . . .	$12.75 x	____	= $ _____

+ tax (for Illinois residents only) = $ _____

+ 15% for S & H = $ _____

TOTAL = $ _____

☐ Check # _____ ☐ Visa ☐ MasterCard Exp. Date ___/___/___

Card # _____

Signature _____